This River Here:

POEMS OF SAN ANTONIO

San Antonio has always been a city of food and culture — una ciudad de cafés llenos de poesía y canción. Here we see some of San Antonio's legendary "Chili Queens" in Haymarket Plaza. A 1933 journalist described this scene: "There is no light on the plaza but that of lanterns and of the distant street lamps, which shine garishly through bottles of highly colored soda pop along the tables…. Someone is sure to have a guitar. Proprietors of various tables pay the musicians with food to sing." The popular chili stands were first located mainly in Military Plaza, but moved to Market Square when the "Bat Cave" city hall was built there in 1889. When the Municipal Market House — El Mercado — was built in 1900, they moved west to Haymarket Plaza and Milam Park. And through it all runs "This River Here." Libraries Special Collections from the Institute of Texan Cultures.

POEMS OF SAN ANTONIO

Carmen Tafolla

First Poet Laureate of San Antonio

WingsPress

San Antonio, Texas
2014

Cover and author photographs, and
photographs on pages viii, 46, 69, 75 and 77 by Bryce Milligan.
Photographs on pages 50-51, 74 and 80 by Carmen Tafolla.
Photographs on pages 3, 6, 14, 16, 30, 54, 58 and 61 are property of the Tafolla family.

First Edition

(Paperback) Printed Edition ISBN: 978-1-60940-399-7
ePub ISBN: 978-1-60940-400-0
Kindle/MobiPocket ISBN: 978-1-60940-401-7
Library PDF ISBN: 978-1-60940-402-4

Wings Press
627 E. Guenther
San Antonio, Texas 78210
Phone/fax: (210) 271-7805

On-line catalogue and ordering:
www.wingspress.com
All Wings Press titles are distributed to the trade by
Independent Publishers Group
www.ipgbook.com

Library of Congress Cataloging-in-Publication Data:

Tafolla, Carmen, 1951-
[Poems. Selections]
 This River Here: Poems of San Antonio / by Carmen Tafolla, First Poet Laureate of San Antonio.
-- 1st ed.
    pages. cm.
  ISBN-13: 978-1-60940-399-7 (pbk. : alk. paper) -- ISBN 978-1-60940-400-0 (ePub ebook) --
ISBN 978-1-60940-401-7 (Mobipocket ebook) -- ISBN 978-1-60940-402-4 (pdf)
  1. Mexican Americans--Poetry. 2. Hispanic Americans--Poetry. 3. San Antonio, Texas--Poetry. 4.
San Antonio, Texas--history. I. Title.
  PS3570.A255 T48 2014
  811'.6--dc23   2014007524

Contents

1.

*Listen to the voices in this breeze,
your ancestors, the trees
the river that remembers . . .*

II.

The Mestizo Molcajete's Mezcla

III.

A Site to See Deep Time

A Note on the Use of Italic Type:

In general, it is the practice of both this press and this author not to use italic type to distinguish between English and Spanish, as we believe that the "Tex-Mex" of our region represents a specific bilingual dialect, developed over the last two centuries. However, oral presentation of these poems often places emphasis on certain words in the text, some of them in Spanish. We have chosen to emphasize those instances by using italic type. The decision to use a Spanish word often comes along with an implication that the word is set apart, elevated in importance. Where Spanish words occur without italicization, the oral emphasis should be equal to that of the English context. Where italicization occurs, be it in English or Spanish, it may indicate a word's special status within a cultural context, or it may simply indicate a different speaker or an emphasis within that particular text.

Para mi pueblo

"Bathing in the San Antonio River,"
Frank Leslie's Illustrated Newspaper, *January 15, 1859.*
This scene was described by a visiting German scientist, Dr. Ferdinand Roemer,
who passed through San Antonio in 1846.

1.

Listen to the voices in this breeze,
your ancestors, the trees
the river that remembers . . .

This River Here

This river here
is full of me and mine.
This river here
is full of you and yours.

Right here
(or maybe a little farther down)
my great-grandmother washed the dirt
out of her family's clothes,
soaking them, scrubbing them,
bringing them up
clean.

Right here
(or maybe a little farther down)

Washing clothes on San Pedro Creek, ca. 1900. Photographer unknown.

Reverend M.F. Tafolla, baptising parishioners in the river, c. 1933.

my grampa washed the sins
out of his congregation's souls,
baptizing them, scrubbing them,
bringing them up
clean.

Right here
(or maybe a little farther down)

my great-great grandma froze with fear
as she glimpsed,
between the lean, dark trees,
a lean, dark Indian peering at her.

She ran home screaming, "¡Ay, los Indios!
Aí vienen los I-i-indios!!"
as he threw pebbles at her,
laughing.
Till one day she got mad
and stayed
and threw pebbles
right back at him!

After they got married,
they built their house right here
(or maybe a little farther down.)

Right here,
my father gathered
mesquite beans and wild berries
working with a passion
during the Depression.
His eager sweat poured off
and mixed so easily
with the water of this river here.

Right here,
my mother cried in silence,
so far from her home,
sitting with her one brown suitcase,
a traveled trunk packed full with blessings,
and rolling tears of loneliness and longing
which mixed (again so easily)
with the currents of this river here.

Right here we'd pour out picnics,
and childhood's blood from

dirty scrapes on dirty knees,
and every generation's first-hand stories
of the weeping lady La Llorona
haunting the river every night,
crying "Ayyy, mis hi-i-i-ijos!" —
(It happened right here!)

The fear dripped off our skin
and the blood dripped off our scrapes
and they mixed with the river water,
right here.

Right here,
the stories and the stillness
of those gone before us
haunt us still,
now grown, our scrapes in different places,
the voices of those now dead
quieter,
but not too far away . . .

Right here we were married,
you and I,
and the music filled the air,
danced in,
dipped in,
mixed in
with the river water
    ... dirt and sins,
    fear and anger,
    sweat and tears,
    love and music,
    blood.

And memories . . .
It was right here!

And right here we stand,
washing clean our memories,
baptizing our hearts,
gathering past and present,
dancing to the flow
we find
right here
or maybe —
a little farther
down.

*Newlyweds Ernesto Martínez Bernal
and Herlinda Marroquin Bernal,
in Brackenridge Park, ca. 1937.*

There've always been rattlesnakes

especially if you live in Texas,
quietly coiled potent surprises
filled with regrettable poisons
scorpions startled under rocks
tails poised for incisive action
flash floods submerging the floor, the bed
wiping away anything not rooted yards deep
droughts that wilt the cactus,
bake the trees, suck dry the elderly

there've always been rattlesnakes,
husbands collapsed to the ground, stores gone broke
grandmothers fading away, bills eating the grocery money,
heart attacks at midnight, heat strokes at 4 p.m.
wagons, cars, bikes, crumpled into broken skeletons
tornados that wreak havoc, lightning that incinerates homes into black ash
cancers that appear when least expected,
disasters that life or nature makes

But even the cruelly unexpected fangs of rattlesnakes
grow brittle over time
crumble into the offended earth
even droughts bathe eventually in the abundant August chubascos
even long-staring skeletons become rich abono
fertilizing the persistent pecan trees
          the hope-filled shoots of chile serrano
          the motivation of survivors trying to rebuild
              bone by desperate bone
              to rebuild

Survival Instructions: Summer, 103°

Feel yourself sizzle on the streets
    Sizzle on the streets
        Sashay sassy as salsa
            Slip survival into sunglare like a native
              Toughen up the soles
                 Strengthen the heart muscle
                   Reinforce the mind with steel and sunrise
             Drink more water
         Bless the air conditioner
        Fry your huevos rancheros on the sidewalk
      Sweep the schedule, Clear space for the wake
Hand a dollar to the homeless man on the corner
  holding his bright blue windshield cleaner spraybottle
    wiping circles in the empty air
      hoping for a yes
         some coins
           a bed
        Lasso the chaos of your collapsing life like a lost steer
      Wrangle it with this well-worn rope
    made to survive the torrid heat
the chaparral of baked dirt
    the creeping cancer of years peeled to bone
      Feel yourself sizzle on the streets
            Sizzle on the streets
                Sashay sassy as salsa

Warning

Don't smell the smoke of a brown ghost
who keeps starving white
and dying brown.

He causes *mitotes* like a Texan Indian
and then goes through the winter
sucking on cactus skins and searching
for overlooked mesquite beans
gone brown.

Instead he finds Spanish missionaries too
eager to adore him, and nations too
foreign to respect him, but only one
or two
mesquite beans.

Wind

Like the breath   of a dying person
you fear it's   gone for good
until an erratic drag   on the oxygen around you
pulls more life   out of what's left
That's the way it is   sometimes
especially in the   heat of August
and not enough air   to think clearly anyway

Wind changes here like the moods of a toddler,
extreme and sudden, fierce, difficult, but always innocent,
an overwhelmingly ominous Chubasco,
that magic moment, that season in minutes
when the sky dresses in black to scare you but instead
Wind excites you, warns you, whispers shivery change
into your ear, points to clouds heavily pregnant with
drops ready to fall, to pour, to crazily conquer everything
in gleeful, unrestricted abundance, wild and without caution
on a joyride of ecstasy with a Wind you are starting to
fall in love with . . .

Then, She changes.   Still, but not static
Charged with potential, holding sparks of danger,
pain, power, beauty, the promise of
ice, maybe the miracle of
snow, surely the sharp comfort of
cold, a flesh-stunning contrast to the sweet-burning
fires, which also blow wind, of a different face

She doesn't stay this way
(like the saying goes, if you don't like the weather
in Texas,   just wait a minute.)
Wind of spring or late fall
even midwinter and if you're lucky summer
is most often quick and sweet, rejuvenating
young and playful, pleasant, refreshing
against the persistent heat of the sun
Whipping through in laughter
She reminds us of the canyons of deep time
the adobe structures of our heritage
our kinship to the river, to the love-filled wildflowers
her cousinship to clouds, to trees, to the
air borrowed in our lungs, borrowed and recycling
constantly, life to life, origin to origin
The blowing mane of our vibrant mother
her breezes kiss this planet
with every movement
every toss of her voluptuous locks

City of Wings

(A word pantoum in centuries)

eagle floats low on the wingpath between clouds
dips on the cool cradle of the rippling river
visions resting place in the laughter of the pecan trees

children of the pecan, of roast rabbit and sacred deer, cradle
firstbabies, weave reeds together with laughter, dip gurgling water
from springs, breathe vision from the sweet wings of home

"Camp of the Lipans" (partial image) by Theodore Gentilz, 1840s.
Courtesy of the Witte Museum, San Antonio, Texas.

*"San Pedro Spring", ca. 1850, lithograph from a drawing by Hermann Lungkwitz,
and "drawn in stone" by E. Friedrick Rau & Son, Lithographers.
First published in* San Antonio de Bexar, *by William Corner (1890).*

tired strangers, marching through the heat, thick brush,
weighted down with orders and papeles, steal laughter from the schedule
vision river as aqueduct, pecan cradles as prayer wings folded

covered wagons wing in immigrants visioning land
new cradles, new lives, laughing pecan groves
settle, promise allegiance, stake out corners of wooden homes

captive warriors, eagle feathers cradled tenderly in their hands
their own wings clipped and laughter swallowed, search pecan horizon
request deer and wildlife brought to fort, to still vision a world of fair hunting

*In 1886, Apache chiefs Geronimo and Natchez with others of their band were
held by the U.S. Army in the Quadrangle of Fort Sam Houston. They requested that
deer and wildlife be brought and left to roam, so that they might hunt and feed
themselves in a more acceptable way. A century later, San Antonio children could
still enjoy the fawns at a "petting zoo" in the Quadrangle that reminded many
old-timers of the Apaches' simple request.*

oppressed eyes search for safety, full stomachs, fair treatment
rock other families' cradles, wash dishes in rooms behind the laughter
dig holes, weeds, gather pecans, vision river fiestas to survive, sprout wings

Lewis Crossing, 1890s. The river was where women gathered to wash clothes.
Black domestic servants worked long hours, long after the Civil War.
San Antonio Express-News, Raba Photograph Collection.

homesick soldiers, shiny wings on chests, cradle memories of home,
tears now touched by aroma of warm pecan laughter,
vision fiesta, passion, peace, a new flavor, romance, home

tiny train, all brightly colored, chugging children of all ages
through the pecans and over the river, cradling small cubes
of laughter, love, enchantment, visions flying like eagle, wings stretched

Eloise May Tafolla and the Castañeda family, ca. 1951,
at one of Dionisio Rodríguez's concrete sculptures, Brackenridge Park.

creatures of rainbow plumage, papel picado colors, cultures, ideas
varied, like Texas wildflowers, seeded of different anthems, skins, tongues
pulled to this place, draped in laughter, cradled in pecan histories, possibilities

wings of laughter and creation spread to full span, freed to reclaim
yesterday, tomorrow, now, to read pecan-carved signs,
cradled visions together — in this city of wings

Aquí

He wanders through the crooked streets
that mimic river beds Before
and breathes the anxious air in traffic
filled with tension left from wooded crossroads in attack

He shops the Windows, happy,
where the stalking once was good
and his kitchen floor is built on bones
of venison once gently roasted.

"It's a good place for a party!" he concurs
to friends now dressed in jeans.
The ground was already beaten smooth
and festive by the joy of ancient dances.

He feels the warmth,
and doesn't know his soul is filled
with the spirit of coyotes past.

River Music

Curving into its cálido colors
mirrored against its own marbled movement
this stream has always sprung simply
smoothly from the heart of song
making soft melodies ring from the leaves
from mission bells and tender voices
of children who play here between the centuries
rippling in and out of laughter

Strong as silt, they stay unchanged
unweakened even by the years
their large dark eyes still staring, boldly
begging miracles of this green liquid gem
that washes quiet through city's soul
healing, hearing, hoping

From sunpeak's sound of rest
a moment's cool peace stolen from
Payaya-speaking trees,
to midnight's festive dance of colors
shimmers on the river singing
weaving past the barges named
María and Elena
and the paddleboats' soft splash,
glimmering through and past
its sons and daughters
grown and multicolored like its flowers, barges,
like its Christmas lights,

comes this river music,
comes this harmony
to make the spirit-breath
dance peaceful
and flow strong,
reflecting
the very rhythm
of you

Ca. 1895. One of the elaborate paddle boats on San Pedro Lake, a body of water immediately
below San Pedro Springs. As early as 1873, Scribner's Magazine praised the park's beer
gardens and other amenities, including a small zoo and a bandstand.. The area was
declared an "ejido" — public or common land — by King Philip V of Spain, in 1729.
Thus San Pedro is the second oldest public park in the United States.
UTSA Libraries Special Collections from the Institute of Texan Cultures.

The San Antonio River at the turn of the century, from the St. Mary's Street Bridge, looking west. The Twohig house is on the right. The buildings on the left front onto Commerce Street. Courtesy of the San Antonio Conservation Society.

Bongo Joe

See him? See him there? Middle o' downtown. Right on that spot!
I do. Sunsparkle, starlight, joylight, drumshine. It's Bongo Joe.
Drumming on everything that makes a sound
Trashcans, oilcans, barrels, cymbal pans
filling for forever this corner with this man.
Just listen to those drums sing your soul happy
Dance the river harmony to *padda rappa bang*

Yeah, we know he's been long dead. Maybe ten,
or twenty years, but we who heard 'im Know
See and Hear and Feel it in our bones
Clang clang, ting ling, tingalong tingding
Holding up a smile, pouring through the tough patch
Hurting, sad or worried, whistling all the while
Hope stirred by a brave and gentle King, assassination only
Caused him to sing *padda rappa tap, bang bong bing*

You wonder why we stop and suck joy deep into our lungs
shake our ribs until they clank, tap feet, roll hips
each time we see this samba-saturated spot
between the traffic lights and clunking, clattering crowds?

Cause we still hear him everytime we pass
We still dance the drumdance with our bones
feel the clang clang reverberate in every car that chugs along
every city bus rattling like those steel cymbal pans
a shuffle shuffle bam rhythm in every shoe that steps on by,
every March, every Move, every breath, every sigh.
Hearts pick up, turn happy to the rhythms floating high

Spot holied by the years of making hearts beat to the drum
to the steel barrel bang and the clong clong cymbal hum
making feet at work or play *tap-tap-a-rap* skip-step in time
Life's sounds breathe away a symphony in mime
Saturday Night Downtown Spirits samba past, joy so fine,
all lights and dance and fiesta, Bongo Joe, right there in line.

George Coleman, "Bongo Joe," 1982, performing on South Alamo Street, between Commerce and Market Streets, his habitual location for almost three decades. An accomplished jazz pianist who once accompanied Dizzy Gillespie, Bongo Joe played his handmade tuned oil barrel drums at the New Orleans Jazz and Heritage Festival nine times. He came to San Antonio for HemisFair '68 and became one of the city's most cherished street performers. He died in 1999. UTSA Libraries Special Collections from the Institute of Texan Cultures.

El Mercado / Farmer's Market

-¡*Molcajetes!*
All ready to be cured
with little grains of rice.
Velvet Pictures!
For your living room, Señora —
Just look at this magnificent tiger here, or here —
Jesús, with his crown of thorns,
Or President Kennedy
(he was so good to us Mexicanos)
Get it for your comadre – the one that's so involved
in las neighborhood meetings!

"EXCUSE ME – DO YOU HAVE SOM-BRAY-ROES?
THOSE GREAT BIG ONES, YOU KNOW?"

-¡Chiles!
Fresh, hot, (and at a good price)
¡Chile Petín! ¡Serranos! ¡Jalapeños!
¡Chile Colorado, all ground up already!

"EXCUSE ME – ARE THESE HOT?"

-It feels so hot already. It's bugging me.
My father used to call these days La Canícula, the Dog Days.

-Y La Tencha? Why isn't she here today?
Did she miss her ride?

-Oh, you didn't hear? Eeeee — what a tragedy!
Well, it's that her brother—the one that lives with her—
went to the Social Security office
so he could get paid his retirement,
and that they can't pay him, they say, because his boss
hadn't taken out anything for Social Security
after 40 years.

Pedro Franco, one of the farmers who sold vegetables at El Mercado.
Libraries Special Collections from the Institute of Texan Cultures.

And that his chest is hurting him
but he doesn't want to go to the doctor
because he doesn't have the with-what, you know?
And he's still not sixty-five
for Medicare—
so he just kept quiet and took it,
and didn't complain no more

"IS IT FAR FROM HERE TO THE ALAMO?"

-And that yesterday when Tencha gets home
with that big ole mountain of paper flowers in her arms,
the ones she sells, you know, and that the gringos
like so much,
well, on getting inside the door,
loaded down with everything and not seeing what was there,
that she stumbles on the body of her brother
on the floor, and she falls on top of him
flowers and all.
And the poor guy deader'n a …
Well! That La Tencha feels like dying of *pena*
que why didn't she make him go to the doctor
and pay it for him,
in little down payments or something,
like the lay-a-way at the stores, or *algo,*
all feelin bad, poor thing.
What a shame, hombre.
-Yeah, poor Tencha.
Listen, if you go by her house,
bring me the flowers and whatever she has to sell,
and I'll sell them for her here,
so the poor thing has for her expenses.

-Okay, Mano. And the corn and the fruit
That I don't sell today,
I'll take it to her—
After all, que tomorrow is another load.

-Yeah, tomorrow is another load.
A-ay, that's life.

-That's life.

-¡Molcajetes!
All ready to be cured
with little grains of rice.

Poets Cecilio García-Camarillo, Reyes Cárdenas, and Carmen Tafolla,
in front of El Titán Tortillería, 1976. Photograph by César Augusto Martínez.

Allí por la Calle San Luis

West Side — corn tortillas for a penny each
    Made by an ancient woman
      and her mother.
    Cooked on the homeblack of a flat stove,
    Flipped to slap the birth awake,
    Wrapped by corn hands.
Toasted morning light and dancing history —
    earth gives birth to corn gives birth to man
    gives birth to earth.
Corn tortillas — penny each.
    No tax.

The family of Avelina and Anastasio Hernández,
in front of their house, ca. 1914, with six of the nine children
they would eventually have. A manual laborer, Anastasio died young.

Fragile Flames

Altares viejos of my path-warmed house
older than our prayers
light as sacred sunrays
rich as scarred and ancient wood
your votive one-day candles last
well beyond twilight, stubborn miracles
on this inherited dark wool sarape
with stained and balding fringe
still tipping stripes of life's
most painful, hopeful colors

tiny lights make loans of faith
to midnight's darkest storms
My people
lean on a chance
live on a hope
pray in a fragile flicker
of stolen candlelight

Holy places around us everywhere
tiny hallway tables with a handtorn branch
of esperanza-yellow bloom and seeds
dressertops with tin milagro wings
backyard carefully historied pile of stones
each one a prayer a bead of sweat
protecting red-dressed, star-cloaked Virgin
a now-unsainted Christopher
nervous on the dashboard
with the cross flying above him,

the doilied corner shelf with pictures
of those lost six months or sixty years ago
still with us

These resilient rocks of lifepath prayers
wet-mortared of the past and present
always bow to possible milagros living in the future
Their flowers — living, dead, or artificial — faithful
testifying silently to our belief
that fragile flames
soft-speak the power
of things too real
too strong too deep
to be simply
seen

Altar para los Muertos, San Antonio, Texas, 2013.

San Antonio

They called you lazy
They saw your silent subtle screaming eyes
And called you lazy
They saw your lean, bronzed workmaid's arms
And called you lazy
They saw your centuries-secret sweet-night song
And called you lazy

San Antonio,
They saw your skybirth and sunaltar
Your corndirt soul and mute bell toll
Your river ripple heart, soft with life
Your ancient shawl of sigh on strife
And didn't see

San Antonio,
They called you lazy

Our Abuelos, the Trees

Our Abuelos, the trees, stand guard,
their bark-lidded eyes, tired from too much wisdom,
have seen a thing or two.
They sometimes sit so still
we don't even see them
Always, they see us
squint those wooden curandero eyes
at foolish grandchildren so so
young they think that they
discovered this place
discovered history
discovered life.
Los Abuelos laugh among themselves
shake their heads, leaves tossed like greying locks
tremble in a deep breath
settle in for another siglo or two
and hope the grandchildren
won't tear up the place too much in the meanwhile

Our Abuelos, the trees, hum low lullabies around us
whisper words of warning beside us
hope we'll eventually grow up enough
to learn to speak the language
or at least learn how to behave
when spoken to

Seeds

This sun-splattered ground takes seeds
and makes them bloom like blessed weeds
grow like sky awakening, pulse
to deepest drumbeat dreaming
while a mother
plants

This riverbending alma blends and folds
sprinkles cross-cultura abrazos through a Fiesta crowd
cracks cascarones, multicolored joy, like tiny fireworks
makes us laugh when we might cry, wear coronas with *orgullo*
feel like the royalty
it knows us to be
while a mother
plants

This swath of gentle earth lets rise the steam of centuries,
this breath of peace and song of celebration,
this kiss to earth and sky, to human laugh,
cariños tossed into the saintly breeze of spring,
the softest spirit of the silt
the undisputed power
of the sun
while a mother
plants

A single mother plants her twins here,
feeds them shared morsels of sweet justice,
cool dreams of change, and daily *ollas de herencia*

The miracle of sustenance bears fruit
birthed from work and poverty,
fed on stubborn siglos of survival,
bred to open streams of sunshine,
doors of possibility, soil filled with promise
where other mothers also then
can plant their seed

This place of peace
this breath of hope
this fertile crumbling handful
this place where
a mother
plants

Feeding You

I have slipped *chile* under your skin
    secretly wrapped in each enchilada
    hot and soothing
    carefully cut into bitefuls for you as a toddler
    increasing in power and intensity as you grew
    until it could burn
    forever

    silently spiced into the rice
    soaked into the bean caldo
    smoothed into the avocado

    I have slipped *chile* under your skin
    drop by fiery drop
    until it ignited
    the sunaltar fire
    in your blood

I have squeezed cilantro into the breast milk
    made sure you were nurtured with
    the clean taste of corn stalks
    with the wildness of thick leaves
    of untamed monte
    of unscheduled growth

I have ground the earth of these Américas in my molcajete
    until it became a fine and piquant spice
    sprinkled it surely into each spoonful of food
    that would have to expand to fit your soul

Dear Mijo Dear Mija
Dear Corn Chile Cilantro Mijos
This
is your *herencia*
This
is what is yours
This
is what your mother fed you
to keep you
    alive

11.

The Mestizo
Molcajete Mezcla

Both Sides of the Border

that deep delicious desire to run on two tracks   at the same time, jump back
and forth or let one foot fall inside each track   like a little girl straddle-
skipping two sides   of a curb
to read the subtitles   in Spanish and
hear the English words   simultaneously
to write one   story in the
legal lines of the legal pad   and then to escape and scribble illegal notes
up the margin on a whole different   page
or poem   or poema.

I was born bilingual—   a lullaby between the
Tex and the   Mex —
my first nickname an admonition   to a tío, primo hermano de mi papá,
as he painted the walls of my house   perched high on a ladder
Man Caes, I shouted,   a name I'd call him forever after, and he me,
our bond, our new language   never as correct as expected
Never Te vas a caer, hombre   or even, You're gonna fall, man!
But even then I loved the   octopus arms of my mother language
Tex-Mex, even then I could   not stay within the required lines
not jump the border   not quite step on a crack, break your mother's back,
not live on both   sides
of the border

to be deste lado   y dese lado
to skip-   straddle the curb
one foot   falling on this side
next foot   falling on the other
but more fun when I   rode the curb, balancing above
the world of   territories owned

laughing in my   freedom from either
and both

we were free   from Mexico
not even bound   by their laws
but to prove we were not   conquered property of the U.S.
we sassily insisted on still   saying "La Capital"
not for Washington DC   but for Mexico City.

My tongue runs to jump the language boundaries   sampling like a
gleefully wild child, of the goodies spread out   on both tables
all stuffed into the mouth at once by fingers,   no forks, no limits, no portions
all impulse.   You can run, you can get away
The viejita watching the desserts   can't catch you
You are sin verguenza,   high and high-powered
wound up with the freeness   sin zapatos
without limits

I write two   novels at the same time
I take two   languages, savor them with no restrictions
no one   measuring portions
I stuff myself   with tasty words of
opposing   origins.

I laugh, am unbroken: the donkey who still rears up
on hind legs to jump over the log   instead of lifting
one leg at a time, ladylike, to be gentle   for passengers.
No, forget your hats, hang on to your seats   the ride is wild, it's
not guaranteed, it's not even defined.   You don't know which
of the two dictionaries   to use.
Like life and death, it gets all   tangled together.
Maybe you're hearing me talk,   maybe you're hearing yourself
maybe I answered a question,   maybe I gave two different answers
like, which religion am I?   *Well, kind of Catholic, pero sin papeles*

since I was born and baptized   a barrio Protestant. Well okay, you say,
let's write down Christian   that ought to define it.

Well, no, I say, *like what I*   *am mainly is*
Native American   *Guadalupana*
you frown at   begin to study
the picture on   my wall of the Virgin of
Guadalupe   *alias Indian Tonantzin*
Um, mixed with   *Sephardic Jew.*
You check for   papers.
No, I explain   *all unofficial, of course.*
I'm a mojada.   *I don't got papers.*

But I do got citizenship   two of'm.
Like I got ownership.   Without the deeds.
These places are mine.   These spaces are mine.
These borders are mine.   Both sides of the river.
It's not that I don't belong.   It's just that I
belong twice.   Don't we all?

It is time.   It is more than twice past the time.
I want an altar.   No, two.
I take the two wooden boxes   once drawers in a work table
in my garage, hit by a tornado   garage torn down, then rebuilt.
The table isn't   there anymore.
That's okay.   Everything has at least two lives.
I can hang them by their   handles. One will be an
Altar to Lupe, the pregnant virgin   (Well, most things *are*
medically possible   aren't they?)
The Catholic Holy Mother   with unborn mestizo baby
Moon, Sun, Gold Stars in cloak   Red dress, Black belt of
Pregnancy, identical to   Aztec Goddess Tonatzin

A Spanish plot? To convert Indians to Catholicism?
No, an Indian plot To convert Catholicism to Indians
Subversively they called her Queen of the Americas,
Her only Crown the Indian Sun, simultaneous with a
Footstool Moon, her hands folded humbly, no one's fooled
I'll keep her big bright Mexican Colors, Green and Red with gold stars
But maybe I'll add something — Blue jeans? Dreamcatcher earrings?
Green card?)
Maybe not.

We pray to her She prays to someone else, maybe to us?
Please, Virgencita… Please, non-Virgencitos . . .
Protect us we say Attack, she says, Charge ahead for yourselves

So the other box drawer, altar
Will be a Dia de los Muertos
I'll call it All My Children, like the soap opera, with the
ad from the soap opera pasted behind it
and pictures of all my kids, even the ones who weren't
born Children, the very sprouting of
life but in the middle of Dia de los Muertos, the very sprouting of
death And like in every Day of the Dead altar, everyone in it will
be a muertito a little laughing skeleton.

So there will be my kids, all of 'em
The live muertitos and the dead muertitos.
All with sweatsuits from Old Navy, or Ross, or the Dollar Store
in different colors and their initial on it
And also mis books and ideas and ancestors, and a bunch of other
people who aren't my children but
could've been and a globe of
the world.

Drawers   altares
in my home   two, so you never get too serious about
just one   never get too committed to
one ideology   one language
one focus   one religión.
My bicultural   bi-altares:
one to an Aztec   Christian
pregnant   virgin.
And one to   all the dead we've
loved before

Hung together, to life   and to death
Or is it, to death   and to life
Or is it,   both things
at the same   time
in both   places
always both sides   of every

          border

De Volada Insurance ... Faster than a Flying Chancla!

The Signs of San Antonio

Drive through these streets
Or better yet, walk.
You will encounter alien worlds
that don't even lift an eyebrow here
Billboards, store windows, signs on a closed door,
graffiti on train cars, even family history that records,
"Your parents met at El Burrito Bar."

"El Patrón's Tire Rental"
"Juan in a Million"
"Porky's Burgers y MAS"
"Pancho Villa Tacos — Got Tacos?"

Witness "De Volada Insurance —
Faster than a flying Chancla"
"El Rey Feo Scholarship Fund" and
"No Alcohol or Bar-B-Q Allowed in this Park"

"El Divino Salvador United Methodist Church"
"Pronto Pawn — We Buy Guns — Closed on Sundays"
"Doo or Dye Hair Salon"
"Chicanos United — Alamo Chapter"

And even if you drive south to get out of town
the news on Texas Public Radio 89.1
begins to be punctuated with conjunto acordión
coming in and out

at all the highway high points
competing for reception
La Lupe 89.1, Rio Bravo, México, plays
"Solo La Mano de Dios Podrá Separarnos"
and "Where o Where Can my Baby Be"
in perfect Spanish translation
and after a while, it all sounds
like the same channel.

John Juan Café, Colorado Street.

San Anto's Mezcla Mágica

What it means to co-exist,
to bloom together,
is that the lines grow fuzzy,
optical illusions with two different faces
appearing at different times
there is not a street that marks
a neighborhood others have not
crossed into
eaten, loved, lived in, tasted in a different way

Even in Alamo Heights,
tamales end up on the "Old Texas" families'
Thanksgiving tables, while "Graciela's" sells
designer suits in sarape colors
Even on Nogalitos Street
the Chinese tamarind seed is the top-selling snack
at the Mexican food counter,
Indian curry gets scooped up
in comal-warmed pita bread
Vietnamese eggrolls brim out of
toasty tortillas made from
German-milled white flour

At the corner of French and Fredericksburg Road
Martínez Barbacoa pairs steaming barbacoa
with ice-cold, carbonated Big Red,
imports El Milagro tortillas from Austin
and Virgin of Guadalupe wooden bracelets from Mexico,
stacks avocados just lusciously ripe enough

but not too soft, in front of the lusciously Olympian Aztecs
posed on a calendar that only distantly layers
echoed rhythms of the Aztec Calendar

After barbacoa and corn tortillas for breakfast
we want "something different" for lunch
and pair black-smoked Jamaican Jerk Bar-B-Q
with chile-roasted corn
So nighttime at Sam's Burger Joint we are not surprised
when in the Music Hall out back
a tall, blonde Chicana named Patricia Vonne
(née Rodriguez and freshly back from concert tour of Europe)
rattles the cage of the stage and
sings a blend smooth as honey
to the harmony of a rock electric guitar
country fiddle
and Spanish castanets

*Members of the family of artist Kimi Jingu, on the
steps at the Japanese Tea Garden (later the Sunken
Gardens). Kimi and Miyoshi Jingu maintained the
gardens, lived in the park, ran the concessions, and
raised eight children. Kimi died in 1938, and the
family was removed at the beginning of World War II.*

What to Say to Your Chicano Lover of 25 Years

A metaphor of place.

You feel better than the dawn-gold pyramids, honey.
You get me higher than the top stone
of the Pyramid of the Sun!

You taste as sweet and spicy as *mole*
hand-picked fresh from the Mercado,
made from ingredients secret-grown in wild gardens.

Your color is as rich as masa para tamales,
and the warm pull of your latidos is as strong as
un tecito from potent hierbas only curanderas know!

Your touch has more magic than that stardance night 25 years ago,
and your shoulders dance me a cumbia, a polka,
and a slow, senses-drunk bolero all in one.

You sana, sana, colita de rana my corazón
Your eye ignites the luminarias of my soul
and I will rise, rise, like hot tortillas rising on a comal, by your side forever.

Yes, the edges of the volcano may now be rough and cold
with scars of rock jagged by fire's distant memory
El Popo's shape has changed, and Ixta's peaks eroded

Yet deep within the core, the rumbling is still strong,
and the hot liquid lava still flows ready
and passionate
as ever.

a swirling confluence of voices   dances up through tree branches and
into the white clouds where   something in the wind gives my lungs
new air   my eyes new   dizzy like shaman dreams   i study
your face   all different-colored and strange-featured   your clothing
so strange   we are closer even than in battle   when horse against
horse and knife against shield we   thunderbreath anger into each
other   i study you now   no anger not even fear   something more
intoxicating   like sharp naked hope on an icy pink dawn   or the first
angry cry of a slippery wet newborn   something new   not familiar   open
to the arms of the sky   like the chaos of holy   ground
we have heard each other's shouts before   warcries   and screams
the peeling off of attachment to life   taunts to death and   still   those
kinds of shouts are   possible   maybe   probable   but maybe
these shouts we give today   of dancing celebration   sweet

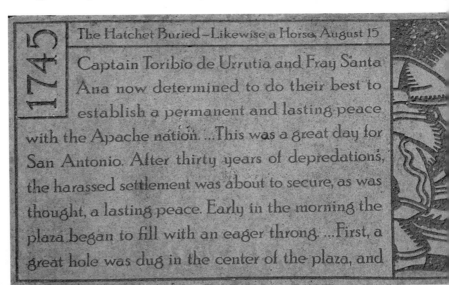

1745

The Hatchet Buried—Likewise a Horse, August 15

Captain Toribio de Urrutia and Fray Santa
Ana now determined to do their best to
establish a permanent and lasting peace
with the Apache nation. ...This was a great day for
San Antonio. After thirty years of depredations,
the harassed settlement was about to secure, as was
thought, a lasting peace. Early in the morning the
plaza began to fill with an eager throng. ...First, a
great hole was dug in the center of the plaza, and

peace   open hearts   there is weariness in war   i see it in your
eyes now something i have never seen before in you   never   been so
close to taking   your hand   we dance   around this hole
you in your uniform and I in mine   the hole we've dug in this plaza
holds the hatchet   the arrows   the swords   the guns   the horse
and maybe our enmity   distrust   maybe our bets the other side would
never change   maybe also planted here   the seeds of
hope   of fresh air   human voice   in this shout of desperation plea
for peace   this deepest longing to live without spilt blood   i might be
wrong   we might forget this moment but   still I shout   my lungs the
breadth of the sky   my hunger for new strange friendship   wide too
we dance and shout   together   our families ways hearts
swirling blending   blossoming   becoming some new graft of tree that
sprouts and sings   ah eh ah eh   aaaaaaaaaaaaaaaaaaaaaaaaaah   eh
a song of stubborn hoped   peace
a song of new   beginnings

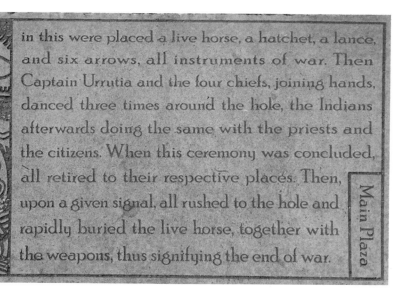

in this were placed a live horse, a hatchet, a lance,
and six arrows, all instruments of war. Then
Captain Urrutia and the four chiefs, joining hands,
danced three times around the hole, the Indians
afterwards doing the same with the priests and
the citizens. When this ceremony was concluded,
all retired to their respective places. Then,
upon a given signal, all rushed to the hole and
rapidly buried the live horse, together with
the weapons, thus signifying the end of war.

Main Plaza

Plaque in front of the Bexar County Courthouse.

Spreading My Mexican Blood

A plastic bag of blood. A small gulf
fed by tributaries. A tube in my puffy vein.
The river flows to the coast. I feel smooth, connected.
-Are you donating blood to find out if you have HIV/AIDS?
-Have you had sex with someone from Africa in the last two years?
-Have you ever received money for sexual acts?
-Have you received a blood transfusion in the last 3 years?
-Have you received a tattoo, illegal drugs, or acupuncture
  in the last twelve months?
Forms filed, bag filled, juice and cookies downed,
I am on the homestretch until Just Short
of the required waiting period, a sudden heat
unlevels my stomach, beads my forehead.
I misplace the air to breathe; they lay me down again.
-Is she a donor, or is she, uh, PAID to do this?

But we Mexicans believe in sarapes — our coat of many colors
Singing racial blends like harmonic mestizajes
we welcome with abrazos the mix, the tying in of family kin
Despite so many people wondering
where we came from why we're here
who are these foreigners, illegals
Not knowing we are centuries-connected to
this unyielding river, this scar of trees, this well-ground dirt
beneath their feet, carrying our bones
We have been here since before the Anchor Baby Washington
was born, before the poor and hungry Pilgrims
crossed over without papers, immigrants without
permission from the standing democratic governments.

Know me now - I am no foreigner to you nor to anyone.
I carry in these funny veins the blood of those who built this place
before the Europeans flaunted flags. I also carry Spanish Arab,
Spanish Jew, Aztec, African, Apache,
Roman soldier, Mayan mathematician, Pueblo,
Basque and Navajo, Goth and Celt, Gypsy Indian from India
and so many uncounted others.
With these tubes, I tie my veins to yours.
I am leaving droplets of myself in you
stretching out this warm and welcoming sarape
spreading my good Mexican blood all over

Fernando Aguirre and Tencha Bernal married on June 11, 1944. In 2013, they celebrated 69 years of marriage. They had eight children. All graduated from high school, two received Ph.D.'s, three received Masters, and all are employed as professionals. They spend time photographing their grandchildren, volunteering at their church, and attending family birthday parties.

Threshhold

This moment
This cool shade of celebration between the days of work and want
This point of crossing into newness and possibilities
This "lazo" of beads and white cross tieing us together in our vow
This sip of steaming sweet *cho-co-la-te!*.

On this moment I say to you there will be greatness ahead
Joy unimaginable. Pain too, I guess, *así es la vida*
But we will make this home a special one,
Someday own our own,
Have children—
Eight or TEN of them!
And they will ALL graduate from high school, maybe even college!
Have jobs
And opportunities never dreamed before.

We will cross into new decades, new experiences.
With love the same
You will see.
This moment will multiply
Abundance doubling, Laughter doubling,
Love quadrupling.
This moment
This threshold.
You will see.
I will make it good for us.
You will too.

By our sweat and struggle, our unshaken faith
By our hardheaded ox-strength
and our sharp-eyed *caminote* of dreams
the sweetness of this pan dulce
the *vals* sweeping us up like a breeze in fertile spring,
will stay with us forever,
into our brittle-boned age and beyond,
into the songs our children will sing
and the heart chords their children will hear

You will see.
As soon as we cross
this threshhold

At the Table of Cariño

In this place of quiet ripples and breeze smooth as buttercream
a place where the river winds slowly around your heart,
centuries of secret spices scent the air, emanate from rock walls,
wave in the sleepy, long-fingered leaves of branches of príncipe dormido

Herencia has a taste here, a flavor hard to lose
Here, the chile piquín blooms in the backyard,
sprouts tiny fire bombs of piquant power
The ancient trees drop a pilón of pecans in your lap
The tender touch of a watering can makes miracles grow tall –
papaya plants and rows of avocados
where they were never meant to be

Here, arms of love embrace the task, roll enchiladas red as
our library, mix in mole and motivos,
roast corn with chile powder and cilantro
Skin of cinnamon bakes buñuelos, naán bread, sweet potato pie
Fingers the fragrance of rosemary fold mushroom crepes,
drizzle lemon over jícama,
stew okra into gumbo
Hands sweet as survival carve Vietnamese eggrolls, chop water chestnuts,
barbecue the brisket till it falls apart
Eyes deep as chocolate craft homemade tamales
giftwrapped in corn shucks and tied with a bow

"¡Juan, ven a com-e-e-er! Ta caliente-e-e-e!"
And "Y'ALL? Hot and READY!"
Parents, spouses, loved ones at ten thousand tables
call at the same moment

Kids gather, lovers snuggle, even BUSINESS colleagues
brighten, glow to steaming plates set before them
while the sweetly sliced red melon waters the mouth
Everyone is salivating, syncopating, celebrating
in one citywide abrazo of nurturance and delight

In a place of quiet ripples and breeze smooth as buttercream
under the shade of our elders, the trees,
where we sit at the table of cariño
hosted by our multiflavored histories,
                          layered like lasagna
                                    baklava
                                    enchiladas a la Oaxaca
                          smoothed and melded like matzo ball caldo
                                    like huevos con wienies,

magic in our mouths,
                    while we tell savory tales between "Pass the tortillas, would you?"
life is reborn in every bite.

A Southside San Antonio sandia harvest celebration, 1942.

Woman Weaving Words

to Naomi Shihab Nye

Soft ribbon braided in your hair
Fiesta ribbons wreathed at your door
Red ribbon round your gate
You welcome the poets
     friends
     young students hungry to create
You Craft the lines
Weave the letters
Feed the words
Push to flight the poems
   birdlings out of the nest
   now free, now flying, now
   graceful messages in the stream
Spread poetry in the air
   that softly circles a Tower
   named for the Américas
Multiply it like loaves
Promulgate it like baby butterflies
   carrying cariño to this comunidad
Braided through with strands of love
Verses in flight
Sometimes touching

A woman weaves words like nestlings set free into the universe
and watches them fly
some ribbon of hope
into the future

Angelina, Anastacia & Emma: A Trialogue of Place
in the 18ᵗʰ, 19ᵗʰ and 20ᵗʰ centuries

Angelina:
Father Sun likes this place.
When he feeds the pecan trees
in the monte, they reach up for him,
and sing to us to rise and grow
The doves coo, the rabbits and raccoons
scurry away to hide
in the safe bosom of Mother Earth which,
this morning,
smells like chile piquín

Angelina, ca. 1700

Anastacia:
At sunset the women in the plaza
make fat corn tortillas and chile con carne
that leaves its aroma even in the rock walls
even when the stalls are closed and everyone
has gone to rest and only
the raccoons come out, their dainty tracks
filled with love
for this place

Emma:
It's the light purple hours of morning again when even the moon
is dropping off to sleep, dawn not even cracked yet, but the
pecanshellers already warming tortillas made of whatever they have —
flour, cornmeal, beans, cactus, chile — praying the 16-hour day
will bring them home with coins for more

Anastacia:
When I was born, all wet and waxy,
the flag said Spain
when I started school, eager to see everything,
the flag said Mexico
when I danced at my quinceañera, glowing,
the flag on this same mission, flying still,
the sun still full as a nectarine, the children still
playing curving Víboras de la Mar, still capturing
with their sweaty arms the giggle-screaming victim,
the old women in dark rebozos still gliding to mass
still covering their penas and their prayers,
the flag said Republic of Texas
When I gave birth to my third child,
begging the partera
to raise him to the window's light,
let this sky bless him,
keep him safe from these armies, and these rabid wars
the flag had stripes and stars, they called it U.S.A.
When I sat by my daughter's side and stroked her head
while she gave birth, another little boy … no food or
wood to warm the house, the dollars were worth nothing
another war had switched the flag, Confederate States,
I was losing count. And by the time that child could walk,
the flag had changed again.

Anastacia Salinas Tafolla, ca. 1864

Angelina:
When I was born, there was no flag.
Humans went by names and families and character
and home was home, and Mother Earth was
owned by no one, only by herself.
But then the others came, the ones who carry flags,

and waved one on a pole, and staked it in the ground
and said this meant they now owned us.
I'd always thought a human was so much more
than just a square of cloth.

Emma:
The ownership still carries on.
They think they own the worker
if they own the company, own the human
if they own the land,
own the land because a square of paper,
or square of cloth, or
gathering of bossy ones
in one small square of town declare
themselves to be the ones
with all the rights.

Emma Tenayuca, ca. 1938

Angelina:
But the rights were never given, sold, or granted. Their
decrees came only from themselves, they never asked
When the earth belonged to the earth, the water
to the water, the trees to the trees, we who lived here
lived beholding only to our mother earth. I remember when
the human, sky, raccoon and dove, pecan branch and buffalo,
spoke to each other, with respect. And shared the rights.
Ours was a different way. The priests then sent me to
their college to do study. I did not tell them that I thought
they should do study with our elders too. They praised
my readiness to learn; I learned it at the hands of Cousin Owl,
Mountain Cat, and Huisache Tree, who learns to live and grow
even from rock. I learned it from fastchanging norther winds and

chubasco clouds who pour their liberated power without warning,
without papers or permission. I learned from them to learn so fast.
I learned to heed their whispers, speak their language,
hear their voices

Anastacia:
The best of what I learned was from the smells, the wet dirt smell
of rain about to burst, or children ready to be born. The acrid smell of
storms to come, trouble brooding in a shallow chest, of men who
ache to leave to war, of crops about to spoil on the stalk. Or
the sweet smell of welcome tables, taquitos made with love,
mountain laurel blooms perfuming every spring, summer river
under lazy-leafed trees, branches offering refuge, respite, recreation
to a world of harmony. The taste of peace. Of satisfied old age. Of
Respeto.

Emma:
My eyes and ears and nose were open. My fingers sensed
the jagged metal of cold prison bars, the textured heat of
family's rebozo, the smoothe and potent pages in a book,
the ripple of warm river water gushing joy and calma.
But where I most could sense this place was in the chest,
emotions in explosion from injustice, passions pouring clear from
love and hunger, heartaches, mind exploding with ideas, images, ideals.
Of plaza, river, kitchen table, child's hungry eyes, father's dignity denied,
mothers silenced, gathering water in a pot. Only spigot leaking, muddy,
flies at center of the lean-to's just a block away from cars that rumble on,
their headlights blind. And victory, sweet justice -- brought so close we
sometimes touch its hem, the sunlight finally on our back and in our
face.

Angelina:
Yes. Father Sun has always liked this place

Angelina, Anastacia, Emma:
Father Sun has always liked this place.
This place. This place
This little monte of our soul
This little plaza of our hearts
This little rippling river, supper table, cloud chubasco, barrio spigot,
principe dormido tree waving in the breeze,
warm tortilla-smelling, *chile* in the air and in the walls,
pecan passion, dove-cooing, love-filled
place

III.

A Site to See Deep Time

The Witte Museum Calls a Meeting of Scholars and Artists
to Discuss Deep Time in South Texas

Something about the way
the water erodes but draws together
the way it makes dirt recycle in new formations,
new colors, new places, calling, shaping, echoing
people, mountain lions, minnows, monarchs
evermoving, endangered

The way this place has always seemed to pull into flow
a *remolino* of *fantasmas* in contrast
some strange *abrazo* of two worlds grappling, embracing
Coastal Plains and Hill Country
Heat Waves and Icy Northers
Apaches and Tejas
Soldiers and Tourists
Mexicans from here, Americanos from Tennessee
New Mestizos
The way things conflict, circle round, meld, evolve
absorb layered histories of earth
coax, romance, court memories of previous civilizations
a sweat lodge of canticles in cyclical movement
syncopated movement of human experience
sensuous movement that blooms into dance
struggle, adaptation, growth
What has taken place in this space?
Pictographs, oldest illuminated text
Rock Art documents. We do not speak the language
But Place
creates its own language

Culture triggers memory, engrains us in the dirt
offers us the ability to metamorphose, belong, blossom
in this place convulsive, transforming, multi-leveled, diverse
always ongoing, its cosmos unstoppable, innocent, stubborn
Opposite forces create a tension dynamic and intertwined
This place by nature mestizo
missions, teepees, forts, *jacales*, condos, ranches
deep drought followed by rampant flood
killing heat cut by blustery cold
Residents who build a batch of bathhouses
dip into coolness, relief,
swim laughing in heat of summer,
bless the river
shrink back, gasp, swim to safety, weep tears of shock
as floods immerse downtown in fall
curse the river, push to close it down
re-discover river, push to rebuild
create a riverwalk, sense some spirit in the silt, stirred

River re-vitalizes
revises   destroys   restores
confluence of community, culture, river
A diversity of life
an abundance of life
in this river
River, a magnet swirling all surrounding forms of life
confluence, contradiction, interdependence, metaphor,
convergence, everlasting, finite, surplus and deficit, cosmos
center
center
center
source
of all

Sitting at the Ice House

Bones soak up time
Mind soaks up friendship
Summer thirst soaks up icy liquid
In the plastic "glass"

Rare moment of rest, after work and
before the work that awaits at home
Parents slump back against picnic
tables, celebrate shade
while children dazzle in and out
of sunshine speckled on the playground fort
The luxury of food at sun's reclining hour
        prepared by someone else
        served on a paper plate
        so plain and pure its power entices

The loud harmony of *chicharras*
taps the baton, the concert begins
ancient pulse-synched entertainment
via Insect Serenade

Intermission — the background hum of
random words, tired muscles,
compassion of compadres
Ecstatic children rise to their royal roles
dogs gulp fallen morsels
our sigh complete as the last bite
is chewed and swallowed

A San Antonio Ice House
where everyone —
dog and insect
food and children
bird and human
tree and heat wave —
coexist
lay aside the differences, disputes
and soak up all the coolness
life can
invent

The Friendly Spot Ice House, 2014, carrying on the San Antonio ice house tradition.

Big Red . . . and Barbacoa

Big Red
Miracle Potion blooms bright
Bubbles up secrets of survival
Perks us even in the sweltering
suffocating heat of hard summer
Made to make the dead rise
              the weak rouse
              the wilted stand up straight
              and sing its glory
Big Red.
Only for the Brave
        the Bold
        the San Antonian.
A tonic for those crazy enough to plunge
ice cold into the sparkling depths
of resuscitation

The special sizzle of
HIGHLY-caffeinated
HIGHLY carbonated
HIGHLY sweetened
soda water
All the stops pulled out to keep us
alive, alert, awake
Thrown down the thirsty throat
like some icy chaser, strong and stinging
through the thick fat meaty rancho taste
of cowhead — *barbacoa* —
cradled in the earth an overnight of steaming

till it falls apart
the savory siglos flavoring its flesh
with wild monte, mesquite wood
vaquero culture, communal feast
De barba a cola,
from head to tail, nothing wasted,
nothing left to slump under the sun
All energy recycled
San Antonio Conservation-Sweet Survival —
Big Red . . . and Barbacoa

Only for the Brave

Something about the clouds . . .

the billowing of hope, the abundance of
bursting cotton bolls, the promise of
new creations, roiling, each day, each minute

infinity of clouds, traveling always, always here,
plotting to seed the wildflowers, inflate the dreams,
push the centuries, inspire missions, visions, serenity,
birth the progeny, the paths, the peace

something about the way gentleness of winter sun,
spring breeze, summer streams, fall leaves still clinging, still
green, sings together with the severity of icey-knifed northers
and sizzling-death summers, two sides of the same face

something about the poufs of fresh freedom against blue
comfort, something about the power of black movement in
the chubasco rage of the now, peeling back skin to reveal shivering
naked spirit, raw-er than blood, deeper than breath, blooming

something about this place, about this place
that pulls me in and billows me along, and sizzles, carves, blooms,
breathes, births   infinite possibilities
under this sky

Mitote Spirits: Spurs Fans on the Streets

Long before Chris Columbus landed lost on these shores
before Cortés fell in love with Malinche
or Ponce went to drink from every fountain in his sight
before ol' Cabeza almost lost his cabeza
and instead discovered wisdom as a traveling shaman,
the biggest Fiesta here — *Mitote!* —
spun senses dancing round a savory fire with friends
far into the sparkling night, joy and feasting,
the whole town stardrunk from life's struggles
passion, pain and glee
Shout out your rage
Focus, Spirit Silence
Laugh out your worries,
Wave the hides and sticks
and make the conch shells rattle
Sing, lungs to the sky, and dance
and then collapse

Today's *Mitotes* gather round a SpursGame–Fire,
Living rooms and TV's or arenas with a gang of friends
Scream and Shout and Joy and Feasting much the same
Crying out the pain, shouting out the rage
Grab a cold one, Focus, Spirit Silence, Passions
Then laugh out your worries
Wave the black and silver flags
and rattle clackers, jump in cars, honk and parade
and shout to all the city streets your victory
Sing, lungs to the sky, and dance

and then collapse
Next morning, coffee's free
all over town
at all Valero Gas Stations
where Old *Mitote* Spirits
still hang out

Susie Mendiola's "Altar para Los Spurs," 2014.

Mission San José

The rocks are warm
have had the hands upon them
through the years
with sun to bake in
memories
Gentle, even with
ungentle missions
somehow life got through
to Them,
the priests amazed
that rabbit tasted good
slowed their passion fervor
one San Antonio sunny afternoon
learned to
lope
a bit
and breathe
with warm brown human flesh
touched the rocks in
tenderness
one time too many
ceased to call it mission
as it grew to make itself
home
for all of us.

Searching for Mission San José

Like the old man who's come home and recognized his wife
seen her for her strength at last, her grace a miracle to his tired eyes
The art connoisseur finds the crisp Cesar Martínez photograph
in the garage sale stacks at the back
The doctor drinks in, studies, sighs at, the Dionicio Rodríguez piece,
that once-oddly-stared-at, tree-like bench at the park
The *raspa* man is viewed with some appreciation since
his portrait deepened in our memories, framed in our halls
Researchers write about the chile queens long gone
and even Emma Tenayuca is praised (as long as she
stays dead and far enough away from our low-paid workers
whom she would still be capable of organizing, in a flash)

We allocate funds, renovate,
bleach to white the ancient walls of calm cathedral
make altars gleam and gold attract, and bureaucrats glow proud
to reclaim Early City History (though bulldozing Nation's first
estación en español, a few dawn-pink roses tied on
its barbed metal fence like some *Altar a Nuestros Muertos.*)
Elaborate reports and archeological plans agree
Somewhere here are ruins of the *first* Mission San José,
the oldest one, a building that predates our current gem
Queen of the Missions, Blessed by Franciscans,
Bastion of the Granaries, Rose Window framing Hope.
The *first* attempt destroyed by floods, rebuilt
The relics might be near *three hundred* years in age

We dig. Search. Sweat in the sweet San Antonio sun
Brush off each cherished artifact with care, each breath a

promise of the past. Until the earth unveils her yield.
A structure   Solid   Clear   and   Older than our   dreams
Assured we've found the paths of early priests and mission Indians
we carbon-date, illuminate   Results returned, jaws fall slack
A dwelling yes   The mission no
This house was built
ten thousand years ago
This place   this holy place
where people lived   and loved
and called it Home   held it Holy
before you did   Before
Before

La Clorona's Tattoo

has a firebreathing dragon,
rose tattoo on HIS chest,
echoing her good taste.
Red teardrops drip below the rose,
leaking away life. Vines
surround his pose, beautify his guilt,
decorate her smooth, caramel decolleté.

Took half the light bill to get that
tattoo. And then the food card from
Medicaid ran out a week too soon.
But the kids ate ramen noodles every night,
and the daycare paid the days.
On Saturday they gulped free samples
at the grocery store, and when
her boyfriend took her out to dance,
the brats watched DVDs
until they fell asleep
sprawled on the floor .

There was a tale she's now forgot,
before the TV filled the world to overflow,
leaving no time for centuries-ancient lessons.
Something in the darkest corner
of her blood's memories, or maybe just
of her Gramma's lost last words,
warnings about women who heed

men more than their hearts, about men who
shirk off children, plunge into pleasuregreed,
of villages who lose their soul,
of languages their voice, of children
starved, drowned, beat or bashed,
smothered out of life, small organs crushed,
small bodies tossed in trashcans,
of women's hollow shadows ripped with pain
still searching riverbeds — lifetimes too late —
for innocence, for legacy,
for futures crumbled in the silt,
aching, calling out "My children,
Oh, my children!" to the grains of
dust within their soul-less hands

La Llorona absent-mindedly
rubs her fingers on her empty palms
her history scraped raw
too many tongues stolen like parking spaces,
like opportunities, or places in a blister-soled line,
too many lives voided before their dawn, unlived
like words that never did
pronounce themselves

Opens her cupboard, nothing left
but an empty box of Cheerios
turns the TV on
clicks to a channel where the songs
play fast and loud, drown out the
irksome clinging shadowmemory,
plans her next tattoo.

A Skull, perhaps???
With contact lenses mirroring our faces?
Yes, lenses that reflect the dark, green shivers
of a people's deepest fear, reflecting ripples
like river water too, too murky for those so near
to ever see beneath.

Weeping rose tattoo. San Antonio, 2014.

Counter Clock Wise

Move in clockwise circles only, say the Navajo.
Travel only in the direction of the five winds.
It is the way of our people, our sun, our moon,
the natural law of our universe.

I dance in the way of
the Navajo
spiritmemory swirl in slow circles, clockwise only,
set the right direction, whole and sane,
print the natural order with my feet
journey healthy, as the elders' counsel
normal, as the growth of spring

But then I stop
reverse my path
do what is unthinkable
and contrary
and sure to bring bad fortune
Do what we Chicanos in South Texas do
dancing the
Indianized
Hispanized
Americanized
German polka
in giant counterclockwise circles
in a hall of laughing people floating as they twirl
dancing out their contraire hearts
their unthinkable crazy souls
lives always out of order, on the edge, against the tide

history erased, present turned to ghost, denied
death and danger living at our altars
dancing, praying, laughing, at our side

We have truly come to accept our lot
to see the universe no longer of one mind
always reversing between two worlds
always outside the known pattern
of what is, and what should be

To make up for it, we laugh, merge
twirl against the cosmos, shrug,
turn this counterclockwise circle
to good medicine
Wrong Way, Insane, Crazy but
Good
Medicine
Anyway

Secret Laughter

river river run
take my alma with you
centuries of strength
sifting slowly through our souls
gifting us the ánimo to carry on
to sing your song
to sip your cool joy
your secret laughter
to love
   to love
      to love

river river

run

marked

Never write with pencil,
m'ija.
It is for those
who would
erase.
Make your mark proud
        and open,
Brave,
            beauty folded into
    its imperfection,
Like a piece of turquoise
        marked.

Never write
with pencil,
m'ija.
Write with ink
    or mud,
or berries grown in
gardens never owned,
    or, sometimes,
        if necessary,
            blood.

San Antonio is a young Yanaguana woman

all spirit, strength and spark
her skin a cinnamon summer, an autumn pecan
her eyes steady stars in October's dark sky
arms graceful as weeping willow branches
she unravels her hair
that long dark wave of a river
winding, winding right through our hearts
pouring clear through our dreams
that's when she sings
in ancient rhythms of her native tongue
unconquered tunes twirled like mesquite bark
gnarled like the centuries of river oak
shaping the gentleness of buffalo grass
the wildness of wind
a melody trickling cool as river water

San Antonio is a
young strong
Yanaguana woman
who learned Spanish
and then English
and then Tex-Mex
or German, Vietnamese, Czech, Greek, Karén
and a hundred other flowing tongues
to lull the child to sleep

San Antonio is a
young strong smart
Yanaguana woman

who sings chants calls declaims exalts
in all the languages
of her embroidered rebozo bordado
of colors and cultures
but never once forgets
the hum and the rumble
of her still-growing
reaching
river
roots

San Antonio Chicana poet, Yanaguana woman,
Victoria García-Zapata Klein, 1998. Courtesty San Antonio Express-News.

Abono — rich sodded fertilizer

Abrazo — embrace

Abuelos — grandparents

A'i vienen los indios! — The Indians are coming!

Algo — something

Alma — soul

Altares viejos — old altars

Animo — spirit, motivation

Asi es la vida — such is life.

Ay, Mis Hijos — Oh, my children!

Cabeza — head

Cálido — warm

Caminote — Path (implying huge)

Cariño — affection

Chicharras — cicadas

Chubasco — a sudden downpour, usually unexpected

Comal — cast iron griddle on which tortillas are toasted

Corazón — heart

De barba a cola — from head to tail, ascribed as one of the origins
    for word "barbacoa"

Deste lado y dese lado — from this side and from that side (implication:
    of the border)

Herencia — inheritance

Hierbas — herbs

"¡Juan, ven a com-e-e-er! Ta caliente-e-e-e!" — "Juan, come eat. It's hot!"

Latidos — heartbeats

Luminarias — traditional homemade lanterns that decorate a walkway to a party

Masa para tamales — dough for tamales

Mijo/Mija/Mijos — My son, my daughter, my children

Milagro — miracle
Mojado — wetback
Monte — untamed brush country, wild area not covered by residences
Motivos — motives
Orgullo — pride
Papeles — papers
Partera — midwife
Pena — shame
Pilón — an extra gift not paid for, a lagniappe, baker's dozen
Raspa — snowcone
Rebozo bordado — embroidered Mexican shawl
Sana, sana, colita de rana — a traditional verse to soothe children's
    "ow-ies" into healing
Sandía — watermelon
Siglos — centuries
Sin verguenza — without shame
Sin zapatos — without shoes
Un tecito — a hot tea
Vals — waltz
vaquero — cowboy
viejita — old woman
Virgencita — Virgin (in term of endearment)

Acknowledgments:

No book is born without the aid of *parteras* and a community of knowledge. *This River Here: Poems of San Antonio* is no exception. In fact, its deepest debt goes to the City of San Antonio and its beautiful residents, past and present, who have inspired it and co-created it with their spirit and their strength. Thank you to all the places in this city that still carry the original spirit of Yanaguana — the river, the ice houses, the barbacoa stands, the kitchen tables, backyards, the gatherings of Spurs fans, the bus stops, San Pedro Park, Brackenridge Park, the family gatherings, the *altares*, the neighborhood *leyendas*, the trees, the trees, the trees. Deep gratitude to Bryce Milligan of Wings Press, for being always patient and attentive to detail, always willing to go beyond the mere act of publishing to make every book a uniquely beautiful and high quality *tesoro*.

To my patient family — my husband and best consultant, Dr. Ernesto M. Bernal, always smiling, supportive and loving; my children, whose love has always surrounded me and given me hope; and to my amazing 96-year-old mother and walking encyclopedia of family history. To Velma Nanka-Bruce, whose editing mind is unparalleled, and whose friendship is even more valuable than her editing skills. And to all the friends who buoyed me up during these last 2 years of adventure, challenge, cancer, surgery, and celebration: You have made it an awesome experience! To the staff at COSA, especially Sebastian, Felix, and Diana, you worked like mad dogs to make these crazy dreams and projects in the Poet Laureate Signature Series come true.

To all the duende spirits who whispered menaces in my ear about putting in poems never published before, which captured for SOME San Antonio resident or visitor a special experience they had never seen published in a book — *gracias también, duenditos chulitos y traviesos*. And to all the magazines, journals and anthologies in which some of these poems have previously appeared, thank you. A very brief and inadequate list follows here.

"At the table of cariño" first apperared in *Edible San Antonio*, premiere edition, Fall 2013.
"Survival Instructions, Summer, 103°" in *Huizache*, Fall 2013.

"Marked," an often re-published poem, appeared most recently in *Reflections*, Yale Divinity School, 2013.

"Aquí" and "Warning" was first published in *Curandera*, 1976.

"Allí por La Calle San Luís," another poem that has been published in several places, first appeared in *Caracol*, 1975.

"San Antonio" was first published in *Get Your Tortillas Together*, 1976

"Feeding You" was first published in *Yapanchitra*, Kolkotta, India, 2006.

"Fragile Flames," "What to Say to Your Chicano Lover," and "Spreading My Mexican Blood" were first published in *The Langdon Review*, 2007.

"Wind" was first published in *The Solstice Initiative*, Galway, Ireland, 2013.

"San Antonio is a Young Yanaguana Woman" was first published in *Voices de la Luna*, 2012.

"This River Here" was first published in *The Texas Observer*, 1995, and was included in *Sonnets and Salsa*, 2000.

"Counterclockwise" in *Red Boots & Attitude*, 2002.

Other selected pieces first appeared in *Sonnets to Human Beings*, 1992.

Carmen Tafolla is a native of the West-Side barrios of San Antonio and the author of more than 20 books. Tafolla has been recognized by the National Association for Chicano Studies for work which "gives voice to the peoples and cultures of this land" and has received numerous recognitions, including the Art of Peace Award for "creating art that contributes to peace, justice, and human understanding." She has received the the Charlotte Zolotow Award for best children's picture book writing; the Americas Award, presented at the Library of Congress; two Tomás Rivera Book Awards; two ALA Notable Books; and two international Latino Book Awards. A member of the Texas Institute of Letters, she is currently Writer-in-Residence for Children's, Youth & Transformative Literature at the University of Texas/San Antonio. In 2012, she was named the first-ever Poet Laureate of the City of San Antonio.

Tafolla received her Ph.D. in Bilingual Education from the University of Texas in 1982 and is still doing postgraduate work on her Ph.C. (Curandera of Philosophy.) She lives in San Antonio, Texas with her husband, Dr. Ernesto M. Bernal, her daughter Ariana, her 95-year-old mother, three cats, two computers, one typewriter, a house full of books, a yard full of hierbitas, many dreams, some remedios, and a molcajete.

Other books by Carmen Tafolla:

Poetry:

Get Your Tortillas Together
Curandera
Sonnets to Human Beings & Other Selected Works
Sonnets and Salsa
Rebozos

Fiction:

The Holy Tortilla and a Pot of Beans

Non-Fiction:

To Split a Human: Mitos, Machos y la Mujer Chicana
Recognizing the Silent Monster: Racism in the 90s
Tamales, Comadres, & the Meaning of Civilization
A Life Crossing Borders: Memoir of a Mexican-American Confederate

For Children:

Baby Coyote and the Old Woman / El coyotito y la viejita
The Dog Who Wanted to Be a Tiger
What Can You DO With a Rebozo?
What Can You DO With a Paleta?
Fiesta Babies
and
That's Not Fair! Emma Tenayuca's Struggle for Justice /
¡No Es Justo! La lucha de Emma Tenayuca por la justicia

Wings Press was founded in 1975 by Joanie Whitebird and Joseph F. Lomax, both deceased, as "an informal association of artists and cultural mythologists dedicated to the preservation of the literature of the nation of Texas." Publisher, editor and designer since 1995, Bryce Milligan is honored to carry on and expand that mission to include the finest in American writing—meaning all of the Americas, without commercial considerations clouding the decision to publish or not to publish.

Wings Press intends to produce multicultural books, chapbooks, ebooks, recordings and broadsides that enlighten the human spirit and enliven the mind. Everyone ever associated with Wings has been or is a writer, and we know well that writing is a transformational art form capable of changing the world, primarily by allowing us to glimpse something of each other's souls. We believe that good writing is innovative, insightful, and interesting. But most of all it is honest.

Likewise, Wings Press is committed to treating the planet itself as a partner. Thus the press uses as much recycled material as possible, from the paper on which the books are printed to the boxes in which they are shipped.

As Robert Dana wrote in *Against the Grain,* "Small press publishing is personal publishing. In essence, it's a matter of personal vision, personal taste and courage, and personal friendships." Welcome to our world.

Colophon

This first edition of *This River Here*, by Carmen
Tafolla, has been printed on Edwards Brothers
coated stock containing a percentage of recycled
fiber. Titles have been set in Chaucer type, the
text in Adobe Caslon type. All Wings Press
books are designed and produced by Bryce
Milligan.

On-line catalogue and ordering:
www.wingspress.com

Wings Press titles are distributed
to the trade by the
Independent Publishers Group
www.ipgbook.com
and in Europe by
www.gazellebookservices.co.uk

Also available as an ebook.